100 Interesting Facts About Paris

A Collection of Amazing Facts About Paris

Introduction: Discover the Magic of Paris!

Bonjour, young explorers! Welcome to Paris, the "City of Light", where history, adventure, and surprises are everywhere! From the towering Eiffel Tower to secret streets, Paris is full of wonders.

Get ready for fun, quirky facts that will make you see Paris like never before!

Let's begin our journey through one of the coolest cities in the world!

Chapter 1: History of Paris

- Fact 1: Origins of Paris

- Fact 2: The Name "City of Lights"

- Fact 3: The Roman Roots of Paris

- Fact 4: The French Revolution and Paris

- Fact 5: Paris During World War II

Fact 1: Origins of Paris

Paris began as a small settlement founded by a Celtic tribe called the Parisii around 250 BC. They lived along the Seine River and engaged in trade and fishing. Over the centuries, Paris grew into a major European city, maintaining its roots along the river. The Seine continues to play a key role in Parisian culture, serving as a vital trade route and a scenic backdrop for many iconic landmarks.

Fact 2: The Name "City of Lights"

Paris is often referred to as the "City of Lights" because it was one of the first cities in Europe to install street lighting in the 17th century. It also became a global hub for intellectuals and artists during the Age of Enlightenment, symbolizing the spread of knowledge and culture from the city. This reputation continues today, as Paris remains a vibrant center for art, fashion, and innovation.

Fact 3: The Roman Roots of Paris

In 52 BC, the Romans conquered the Parisii tribe and established a new city called Lutetia, which would later become Paris. The Romans built baths, temples, and arenas, some of which still exist today, like the Arènes de Lutèce, providing a glimpse into Paris's ancient Roman past. The legacy of Roman architecture can still be seen throughout the city, highlighting the enduring influence of this early period in Paris's history.

Fact 4: The French Revolution and Paris

Paris was at the center of the French Revolution, which started in 1789 with events such as the storming of the Bastille, a royal prison. The revolution not only transformed France by ending the monarchy but also left a lasting impact on Paris, with key sites like the Place de la Concorde playing a historic role. The changes initiated during this period set the stage for modern French democracy and reshaped Paris into a symbol of revolutionary ideals.

Fact 5: Paris During World War II

Paris was occupied by Nazi forces from 1940 to 1944, but the city avoided major destruction during the war. In 1944, the French Resistance, along with Allied troops, liberated Paris, marking a significant moment in history, which is still commemorated in the city today with parades and events. The liberation restored Paris's sense of freedom and pride, symbolizing hope and resilience in the face of adversity.

Chapter 2 : Geography of Paris

- Fact 6: Paris's Location Along the Seine River

- Fact 7: Paris's Arrondissements (Districts)

- Fact 8: Climate of Paris

- Fact 9: Green Spaces in Paris

- Fact 10: The Role of the Seine in Parisian Life

Fact 6: Paris's Location Along the Seine River

Paris is situated on both banks of the Seine River, which flows through the city from east to west. This strategic location has historically made Paris a key trading hub and contributed to its growth as a major European city. The river divides the city into two main parts: the Right Bank (Rive Droite) and the Left Bank (Rive Gauche), each with its own unique character.

Fact 7: Paris's Arrondissements (Districts)

Paris is divided into 20 administrative districts known as arrondissements, which spiral outwards from the city center. Each arrondissement has its own distinct identity and attractions, ranging from historic sites to modern neighborhoods. The system helps organize the city's administration and provides a way to explore Paris in manageable sections.

Fact 8: Climate of Paris

Paris has a temperate oceanic climate with mild winters and warm summers. Average temperatures range from about 3°C (37°F) in winter to 25°C (77°F) in summer. Rainfall is fairly evenly distributed throughout the year, contributing to the lush greenery seen in many of Paris's parks and gardens. The city's moderate climate makes it an enjoyable destination for visitors year-round.

Fact 9: Green Spaces in Paris

Despite its urban landscape, Paris is home to numerous green spaces, including parks and gardens. Notable examples include the Luxembourg Gardens, the Tuileries Garden, and the Bois de Vincennes. These areas offer residents and visitors a respite from the hustle and bustle of city life and contribute to Paris's reputation as a green city.

Fact 10: The Role of the Seine in Parisian Life

The Seine River is integral to Parisian life, serving as a major transportation route and a picturesque feature of the city. It has inspired countless artists and writers, and its banks are lined with historic landmarks and charming bridges. The river also hosts popular activities like boat cruises and riverside picnics, making it a central element of the city's cultural and social life.

Chapter 3: Culture and Art

- Fact 11: The Louvre Museum

- Fact 12: Paris Fashion Week

- Fact 13: The Artistic Hub of Montmartre

- Fact 14: The Influence of French Cinema

- Fact 15: Parisian Street Art

Fact 11: The Louvre Museum

The Louvre Museum, located in Paris, is one of the world's largest and most visited art museums. Originally built as a royal palace in the late 12th century, it became a museum during the French Revolution. The Louvre is home to thousands of works of art, including the famous painting Mona Lisa and the ancient Greek statue Venus de Milo.

Fact 12: Paris Fashion Week

Paris Fashion Week is a major event in the global fashion industry, held twice a year in February/March and September/October. It showcases the latest collections from top designers and fashion houses, setting trends for the upcoming season. Paris Fashion Week is renowned for its high-profile runway shows and attracts fashion enthusiasts and media from around the world.

Fact 13: The Artistic Hub of Montmartre

Montmartre is a historic district in Paris known for its vibrant artistic scene. In the late 19th and early 20th centuries, it was the home of famous artists like Pablo Picasso and Vincent van Gogh. The area is famous for its bohemian atmosphere, lively cafés, and landmarks like the Basilica of the Sacré-Cœur. Today, Montmartre remains a popular destination for artists and tourists alike, offering a glimpse into Paris's rich cultural heritage.

Fact 14: The Influence of French Cinema

French cinema has had a significant impact on the global film industry, with Paris as a central hub. The city has been the setting for many influential films and is home to the César Awards, which honor achievements in French cinema. Iconic filmmakers like François Truffaut and Jean-Luc Godard have shaped the world of film through their innovative work.

Fact 15: Parisian Street Art

Paris is known for its vibrant street art scene, with works displayed throughout the city on walls, buildings, and public spaces. The diverse styles and messages of Parisian street art reflect the city's dynamic cultural and social landscape, showcasing a range of artistic expressions that contribute to the city's unique character. This street art transforms everyday urban spaces into open-air galleries, drawing visitors and inspiring creativity.

Chapter 4 : Famous Landmarks

- Fact 16: The Eiffel Tower

- Fact 17: The Arc de Triomphe

- Fact 18: Notre-Dame Cathedral

- Fact 19: The Champs-Élysées Avenue

- Fact 20: The Palace of Versailles

Fact 16: The Eiffel Tower

The Eiffel Tower, completed in 1889 for the Exposition Universelle, is one of Paris's most iconic landmarks. Standing at 324 meters (1,063 feet), it was the tallest man-made structure in the world until 1930. The tower offers panoramic views of Paris from its observation decks and is illuminated with thousands of lights each evening. It has become a global symbol of France and a must-see attraction for visitors.

Fact 17: The Arc de Triomphe

The Arc de Triomphe, commissioned by Napoleon Bonaparte in 1806, honors those who fought and died for France in various wars. Located at the top of the Champs-Élysées, it stands 50 meters (164 feet) tall and features intricate sculptures depicting historical battles. Visitors can climb to the top for a stunning view of the city's major avenues. It also serves as a central point for major national celebrations and events.

Fact 18: Notre-Dame Cathedral

Notre-Dame Cathedral, a masterpiece of Gothic architecture, was constructed between 1163 and 1345 on the Île de la Cité. Known for its impressive façade, rose windows, and flying buttresses, it played a central role in French history and literature. Although it was severely damaged by a fire in 2019, restoration efforts are underway to preserve its historic grandeur. It remains a powerful symbol of Paris's rich cultural and religious heritage.

Fact 19: The Champs-Élysées Avenue

The Champs-Élysées Avenue is one of the most famous avenues in the world, stretching 1.9 kilometers (1.2 miles) from the Arc de Triomphe to the Place de la Concorde. Renowned for its theaters, cafés, and luxury shops, it is also the site of the annual Bastille Day military parade and the finish line of the Tour de France. Its vibrant atmosphere and prestigious stores make it a key shopping and cultural destination.

Fact 20: The Palace of Versailles

Located just outside Paris, the Palace of Versailles is a stunning example of French Baroque architecture and was the royal residence from 1682 until the French Revolution. The palace is known for its opulent rooms, including the Hall of Mirrors, extensive gardens, and the Grand Trianon, a retreat for the French monarchy. Its elaborate design and historical significance attract millions of visitors each year.

Chapter 5 :Food and Cuisine

- Fact 21: The Origins of French Baguettes

- Fact 22: Parisian Pastries (Croissants, Macarons)

- Fact 23: The Café Culture in Paris

- Fact 24: Famous Parisian Restaurants

- Fact 25: French Cheese Traditions

Fact 21: The Origins of French Baguettes

The French baguette, a long, thin loaf of bread, is a symbol of French culinary tradition. Its origins date back to the late 19th century, when it was developed as a practical, easily transportable bread. The baguette became widely popular in the early 20th century, with its crisp crust and soft, airy interior making it a staple in French households and a beloved item worldwide.

Fact 22: Parisian Pastries (Croissants, Macarons)

Paris is renowned for its exquisite pastries, including croissants and macarons. Croissants, with their flaky, buttery layers, have become an iconic breakfast item. Macarons, delicate meringue-based cookies with a variety of fillings, are a Parisian specialty, celebrated for their colorful appearance and rich flavors. These pastries are often enjoyed in the city's many cafés and patisseries.

Fact 23: The Café Culture in Paris

The café culture in Paris is an integral part of the city's social life and daily routine. Parisian cafés serve as meeting places for friends, spots for people-watching, and venues for enjoying coffee and light meals. The tradition of sitting at a café and leisurely sipping coffee while observing street life is deeply embedded in Parisian culture and contributes to the city's relaxed and sociable atmosphere.

Fact 24: Famous Parisian Restaurants

Paris is home to a number of world-famous restaurants that offer exceptional dining experiences. Establishments like Le Jules Verne in the Eiffel Tower and L'Arpège are celebrated for their gourmet cuisine and innovative dishes. These restaurants often feature a blend of classic French techniques and modern culinary trends, drawing food enthusiasts from around the globe.

Fact 25: French Cheese Traditions

France boasts a rich tradition of cheese-making, with hundreds of varieties produced across the country. French cheeses, such as Brie, Camembert, and Roquefort, each have distinct flavors and textures. The tradition of enjoying cheese as part of a meal or cheese course is a key element of French cuisine, reflecting the country's commitment to quality and artisanal craftsmanship.

Chapter 6 :Funny Facts About Paris

- Fact 26: Paris Has Its Own Mini-Statue of Liberty

- Fact 27: Dogs Have Their Own Rights in Paris

- Fact 28: The Paris Catacombs House Millions of Bones

- Fact 29: There's a Nose on the Pont Neuf Bridge

- Fact 30: Paris Has a Phantom Railway Station

Fact 26: Paris Has Its Own Mini-Statue of Liberty

Paris is home to a smaller replica of the Statue of Liberty, located on the Île aux Cygnes in the Seine River. This statue, a gift from the American community in Paris to the French people, stands 11.5 meters (37 feet) tall and faces west toward its larger counterpart in New York. It's a charming reminder of the close historical ties between the two cities.

Fact 27: Dogs Have Their Own Rights in Paris

In Paris, dogs are treated with considerable respect and even have their own designated parks and facilities. Many cafés and restaurants welcome dogs, and there are strict regulations about their welfare. The city also has numerous pet-friendly events and spaces, reflecting the Parisian love for their canine companions.

Fact 28: The Paris Catacombs House Millions of Bones

The Paris Catacombs, an underground ossuary, contain the remains of approximately six million people. Originally quarries, these tunnels were transformed into a macabre burial site in the late 18th century to address overcrowded cemeteries. The catacombs are a popular tourist attraction, offering a fascinating glimpse into Paris's darker history.

Fact 29: There's a Nose on the Pont Neuf Bridge

On the Pont Neuf, one of Paris's oldest bridges, there is a peculiar sculpture of a nose. This quirky feature is a part of a larger piece of street art known as "Le Nom de la Rose," created by artist Thierry Noir. The nose, along with other whimsical elements, adds a touch of humor to the historic bridge.

Fact 30: Paris Has a Phantom Railway Station

Paris is rumored to have a hidden railway station called La Gare de l'Est. Located beneath the city and never fully completed, it was intended to serve as a major transport hub but was never officially opened. The station's existence adds an air of mystery to Paris's already rich tapestry of history and urban legends.

Chapter 7 : Places to Visit

- Fact 31: Musée d'Orsay

- Fact 32: Sacré-Cœur Basilica

- Fact 33: The Luxembourg Gardens

- Fact 34: The Picasso Museum

- Fact 35: The Paris Zoological Park

Fact 31: Musée d'Orsay

The Musée d'Orsay, housed in a former railway station, is renowned for its extensive collection of Impressionist and Post-Impressionist masterpieces. The museum offers a glimpse into the revolutionary art movements of the late 19th and early 20th centuries. Its stunning Beaux-Arts architecture and the transformation of the station into a museum make it a must-visit for art enthusiasts.

Fact 32: Sacré-Cœur Basilica

The Sacré-Cœur Basilica, located at the summit of Montmartre, is known for its striking white façade and panoramic views of Paris. Completed in 1914, it is a popular pilgrimage site and offers visitors a chance to explore its beautifully decorated interior and climb to the top of its dome for breathtaking views of the city. The basilica's location in the artistic Montmartre district adds to its charm.

Fact 33: The Luxembourg Gardens

The Luxembourg Gardens, created in the early 17th century, are a serene retreat in the heart of Paris. The gardens feature beautifully manicured lawns, fountains, and statues, providing a perfect spot for relaxation and leisurely strolls. Visitors can enjoy the picturesque setting, which includes a large pond, flowerbeds, and a historic French-style garden layout.

Fact 34: The Picasso Museum

The Picasso Museum in Paris is dedicated to the works of Pablo Picasso, showcasing a vast collection of his paintings, sculptures, and drawings. Located in the Hôtel Salé, a 17th-century mansion, the museum offers insight into Picasso's artistic evolution and features pieces from different periods of his prolific career. It's a key destination for those interested in modern art and the genius of Picasso.

Fact 35: The Paris Zoological Park

The Paris Zoological Park, also known as the Vincennes Zoo, is located in the Bois de Vincennes and offers a diverse range of animal exhibits. The zoo is home to various species, including lions, giraffes, and rhinoceroses, and features immersive habitats that aim to replicate the animals' natural environments. It provides an educational experience and a chance to see wildlife in a beautifully landscaped setting.

Chapter 8 : Famous Cities Near Paris

- Fact 36: Versailles

- Fact 37: Fontainebleau

- Fact 38: Giverny

- Fact 39: Chartres

- Fact 40: Reims

Fact 36: Versailles

Versailles, located about 20 kilometers (12 miles) southwest of Paris, is famous for the opulent Palace of Versailles, a former royal residence known for its stunning gardens and the Hall of Mirrors. The city played a significant role in French history and remains a symbol of the grandeur of the French monarchy. Visitors can explore the palace grounds and enjoy the beautifully landscaped gardens.

Fact 37: Fontainebleau

Fontainebleau, situated approximately 55 kilometers (34 miles) southeast of Paris, is renowned for its magnificent Château de Fontainebleau, a former royal residence that spans over eight centuries of French history. The château is surrounded by a large forest, which offers excellent opportunities for hiking and outdoor activities. The blend of historic architecture and natural beauty makes Fontainebleau a charming destination.

Fact 38: Giverny

Giverny, located around 75 kilometers (47 miles) northwest of Paris, is best known as the home of the artist Claude Monet. Visitors can explore Monet's former residence and its stunning gardens, which inspired many of his famous paintings, including the iconic water lilies series. Giverny offers a picturesque and peaceful retreat into the world of Impressionist art.

Fact 39: Chartres

Chartres, about 90 kilometers (56 miles) southwest of Paris, is renowned for its impressive Chartres Cathedral, a masterpiece of Gothic architecture. The cathedral is celebrated for its well-preserved stained glass windows and intricate sculptures. The city's medieval streets and historical sites provide a glimpse into France's rich heritage.

Fact 40: Reims

Reims, located approximately 130 kilometers (81 miles) northeast of Paris, is known for its beautiful Gothic cathedral, which served as the coronation site for French kings. The city is also famous for its Champagne production, with numerous vineyards and cellars offering tours and tastings. Reims combines historical significance with a vibrant wine culture.

Chapter 9: Paris's Influence on Science and Innovation

- Fact 41: The Curie Institute

- Fact 42: The Pasteur Institute

- Fact 43: Paris's Role in Aviation History

- Fact 44: Paris's High-Speed Train (TGV)

- Fact 45: The Paris International Exposition (1937)

Fact 41: The Curie Institute

The Curie Institute, founded in 1920, is a leading research center in cancer treatment and radiology. Located in Paris, it is renowned for its pioneering work in medical research and has made significant contributions to the understanding and treatment of cancer. The institute continues to be at the forefront of scientific and medical advancements.

Fact 42: The Pasteur Institute

The Pasteur Institute, established in 1887, is a world-renowned center for biomedical research. It has made groundbreaking discoveries in microbiology and immunology, including vaccines for rabies and diphtheria. The institute remains a leader in research on infectious diseases and public health, continuing to influence global health practices with its advancements and expertise.

Fact 43: Paris's Role in Aviation History

Paris has played a significant role in aviation history, with key events such as the first international flight and the establishment of early aviation companies. The city hosted the 1900 Paris Exposition, where aviation pioneers showcased their innovations. The annual Paris Air Show, one of the world's oldest and most prestigious aerospace events, continues to highlight advances in aviation technology.

Fact 44: Paris's High-Speed Train (TGV)

Paris is the hub of the TGV (Train à Grande Vitesse), France's high-speed rail network that revolutionized travel in Europe. The TGV, which began operation in 1981, connects Paris with major cities across France and neighboring countries at speeds of up to 320 km/h (199 mph). It has set records for speed and efficiency, influencing rail transport worldwide.

Fact 45: The Paris International Exposition (1937)

The Paris International Exposition of 1937 was a major world's fair that showcased technological advancements and artistic achievements. Held at the foot of the Eiffel Tower, the exposition featured groundbreaking innovations and introduced many people to modernist art and architecture. It played a significant role in highlighting Paris as a center of cultural and technological progress.

Chapter 10 : Travel Tips

- Fact 46: Best Times to Visit Paris

- Fact 47: Using Public Transportation in Paris

- Fact 48: Paris's Metro System

- Fact 49: Bicycle-Friendly Paris

- Fact 50: Etiquette Tips for Tourists

Fact 46: Best Times to Visit Paris

The best times to visit Paris are during the spring (April to June) and fall (September to October) when the weather is mild, and the city is less crowded. Summer (July to August) is peak tourist season, with warmer temperatures and larger crowds. Winter (November to March) offers fewer tourists and lower prices but can be quite cold and rainy.

Fact 47: Using Public Transportation in Paris

Paris boasts an extensive and efficient public transportation system, including buses, trams, and trains. The Paris Visite pass offers unlimited travel on public transport and discounts on various attractions. It's advisable to familiarize yourself with the metro and bus routes before your trip to navigate the city smoothly. Additionally, consider using a transportation app for real-time updates and route planning.

Fact 48: Paris's Metro System

The Paris Metro is one of the most efficient ways to get around the city, with 16 lines covering nearly every part of Paris. It operates from around 5:30 AM to 12:30 AM, with extended hours on weekends. The metro stations are well-marked and easy to navigate, making it a convenient option for tourists. Tickets are available at vending machines or kiosks in stations. For a more comfortable experience, consider traveling outside of rush hours.

Fact 49: Bicycle-Friendly Paris

Paris has become increasingly bicycle-friendly, with numerous bike lanes and rental services. The city's layout makes cycling an enjoyable way to explore, with dedicated lanes and bike paths ensuring a safe and pleasant ride. Many popular attractions are accessible by bike, offering a unique perspective of the city. Biking also allows you to cover more ground and discover hidden gems that might be missed on foot.

Fact 50: Etiquette Tips for Tourists

When visiting Paris, it's important to practice polite etiquette. Greet people with a "Bonjour" or "Bonsoir" before starting a conversation, and use "s'il vous plaît" (please) and "merci" (thank you). Tipping is appreciated but not obligatory; rounding up the bill or leaving small change is usually sufficient. Being respectful of local customs and norms will enhance your experience in the city.

Chapter 11: Festivals and Events

- Fact 51: Bastille Day Celebrations

- Fact 52: Paris Plages (Beach on the Seine)

- Fact 53: Nuit Blanche Art Festival

- Fact 54: The Paris Marathon

- Fact 55: Fête de la Musique (Music Festival)

Fact 51: Bastille Day Celebrations

Bastille Day, celebrated on July 14th, marks the anniversary of the French Revolution's storming of the Bastille. Paris hosts a grand military parade on the Champs-Élysées, followed by fireworks near the Eiffel Tower. The day is filled with lively street parties, concerts, and various events celebrating French national pride. Many local restaurants and cafés also feature special menus and events to join in the festivities.

Fact 52: Paris Plages (Beach on the Seine)

Paris Plages transforms parts of the Seine Riverbanks into temporary beaches every summer, typically from mid-July to mid-August. This annual event features sandy areas, sun loungers, and various activities like beach volleyball and pétanque. It offers Parisians and tourists a unique opportunity to enjoy a beach-like experience in the heart of the city.

Fact 53: Nuit Blanche Art Festival

Nuit Blanche, held annually in October, is a city-wide art festival where Paris's museums, galleries, and public spaces stay open all night. The event features contemporary art installations, performances, and interactive exhibits, allowing visitors to experience the city's vibrant cultural scene in a unique nocturnal setting. The festival turns Paris into a dynamic open-air gallery, inviting everyone to engage with art in unexpected places.

Fact 54: The Paris Marathon

The Paris Marathon, held annually in April, attracts runners from around the world to compete in one of the city's most popular sporting events. The course takes participants past famous landmarks such as the Eiffel Tower, Notre-Dame Cathedral, and the Champs-Élysées. The marathon is renowned for its scenic route and festive atmosphere. Spectators line the route to cheer on runners, adding to the vibrant and supportive environment of the race.

Fact 55: Fête de la Musique (Music Festival)

Fête de la Musique, celebrated on June 21st, coincides with the summer solstice and transforms Paris into a vibrant music festival. Musicians of all genres perform on streets, in parks, and in various venues throughout the city. The festival encourages amateur and professional musicians alike to share their music, creating a lively and eclectic soundscape across Paris. The event also fosters a sense of community, as people gather to enjoy and celebrate the diverse musical talents of the city.

Chapter 12: Famous Landmarks and Hidden Gems

- Fact 56: The Palais Garnier

- Fact 57: The Panthéon

- Fact 58: Rue Cremieux

- Fact 59: The Catacombs of Paris

- Fact 60: La Promenade Plantée

Fact 56: The Palais Garnier

The Palais Garnier, also known as the Paris Opera House, is an opulent example of 19th-century architecture. It features a stunning grand staircase, a vast chandelier, and intricate decorative details. The building has inspired numerous works, including a famous novel. Guided tours offer insights into its rich history and architectural marvels. The opera house also hosts a variety of performances, from ballets to operas, enriching Paris's cultural scene.

Fact 57: The Panthéon

The Panthéon is a neoclassical mausoleum in the Latin Quarter, where many of France's distinguished figures are buried. Originally built as a church, it now serves as a national mausoleum and offers panoramic views of the city from its dome. The building's impressive dome and classical design make it a key architectural landmark in Paris. Visitors can explore the crypts of various historical figures, highlighting its historical significance.

Fact 58: Rue Cremieux

Rue Cremieux is a charming, picturesque street in Paris known for its colorful houses and quaint atmosphere. This residential street is often featured in films and is a delightful contrast to the bustling city life. Its charming architecture and tranquil environment make it a favorite spot for photographers and visitors. The street's unique aesthetic and peaceful ambiance offer a delightful escape from Paris's more crowded areas.

Fact 59: The Catacombs of Paris

The Catacombs are an extensive network of underground tunnels that house the remains of millions of Parisians. Opened to the public in the 19th century, they provide a unique glimpse into Paris's past and are a popular but eerie attraction. The labyrinthine passages and macabre displays offer a fascinating and unusual experience. Guided tours delve into the history of these subterranean ossuaries, adding depth to the visit.

Fact 60: La Promenade Plantée

La Promenade Plantée, also known as the Coulée Verte René-Dumont, is an elevated park built on an old railway viaduct. This green space offers a serene walk with views of the city and is a precursor to New York's High Line. The promenade is a peaceful retreat from the city's hustle, lined with gardens, sculptures, and art installations. It provides a unique perspective on Paris's urban landscape and is popular with both locals and tourists.

Chapter 13: Education in Paris

- Fact 61: The Sorbonne University

- Fact 62: Lycée Henri-IV (Top Parisian School)

- Fact 63: Paris's Libraries

- Fact 64: Art Schools in Paris

- Fact 65: The French Academy

Fact 61: The Sorbonne University

The Sorbonne University, established in 1257, is one of Paris's most prestigious institutions of higher learning. It has played a significant role in shaping intellectual thought in Europe and is known for its strong programs in humanities, social sciences, and natural sciences. The university's historical buildings and academic reputation make it a symbol of Paris's educational excellence.

Fact 62: Lycée Henri-IV (Top Parisian School)

Lycée Henri-IV, founded in 1804, is a highly respected secondary school known for its rigorous academic standards and distinguished alumni. Located in the Latin Quarter, it offers an elite education and is renowned for its strong programs in humanities, sciences, and arts. The school has a tradition of academic excellence and intellectual development.

Fact 63: Paris's Libraries

Paris is home to numerous historic and contemporary libraries, including the Bibliothèque nationale de France and the Bibliothèque Sainte-Geneviève. These libraries offer extensive collections of books, manuscripts, and digital resources, serving as important centers for research and public reading. They contribute to Paris's rich literary and academic culture.

Fact 64: Art Schools in Paris

Paris boasts several renowned art schools, including the École des Beaux-Arts and the Paris College of Art. These institutions are known for their comprehensive art programs and their influence on both traditional and contemporary art movements. They attract students from around the world who come to study and develop their artistic skills in the city's vibrant cultural environment.

Fact 65: The French Academy

The French Academy, or Académie Française, was founded in 1635 and is one of France's most prestigious institutions dedicated to the French language and literature. It is responsible for overseeing the French language's development and preserving its purity. The Academy's members, known as "Immortals," are renowned figures in literature and culture, and the institution plays a key role in France's intellectual life.

Chapter 15: Language and Communication

- Fact 66: Parisian French vs. Other French Dialects

- Fact 67: Popular Parisian Slang Words

- Fact 68: The Influence of Latin on Parisian French

- Fact 69: French as an International Language

- Fact 70: Multilingualism in Paris

Fact 66: Parisian French vs. Other French Dialects

Parisian French is often considered the standard form of the language and is the basis for formal French taught around the world. It is characterized by its clear pronunciation and refined accent. In contrast, regional French dialects and accents, such as those from the south of France or Brittany, exhibit distinct variations in pronunciation and vocabulary, reflecting the diverse linguistic landscape of France.

Fact 67: Popular Parisian Slang Words

Parisian slang, or "argot," is a vibrant part of the city's linguistic culture. Common slang words include "bagnole" for car, "kif" for pleasure, and "meuf" for woman. These slang terms often originate from informal or subcultural contexts and evolve rapidly, adding a dynamic element to the language used by Parisians in everyday conversations.

Fact 68: The Influence of Latin on Parisian French

Parisian French has been significantly influenced by Latin, as French is a Romance language that evolved from Vulgar Latin. Many French words, especially those related to law, education, and religion, have Latin roots. This influence is evident in the structure of the language and its vocabulary, reflecting the historical development of French from its Latin origins.

Fact 69: French as an International Language

French is one of the most widely spoken languages globally, with over 300 million speakers across different continents. It is an official language in many international organizations, including the United Nations and the European Union. French is valued for its cultural, diplomatic, and economic importance, making it a key international language.

Fact 70: Multilingualism in Paris

Paris's multilingualism is also reflected in its schools, where students often have the opportunity to learn multiple languages from a young age. Additionally, many public signs, menus, and transportation information are available in several languages, making the city more accessible to international visitors and fostering an inclusive environment for all.

Chapter 16 : Paris and the Environment

- Fact 71: Eco-Friendly Initiatives in Paris

- Fact 72: Green Rooftops and Gardens

- Fact 73: The Paris Agreement on Climate Change

- Fact 74: The Seine River Clean-Up Projects

- Fact 75: Paris's Electric Car-Sharing Program

Fact 71: Son Cubano

Paris has implemented various eco-friendly initiatives to reduce pollution and improve the city's sustainability. These efforts include increasing green spaces, promoting cycling, and introducing stricter regulations on vehicle emissions to improve air quality. The city also aims to become carbon-neutral by 2050, with plans to reduce energy consumption and enhance waste management.

Fact 72: Green Rooftops and Gardens

To combat urban heat and promote biodiversity, Paris encourages the installation of green rooftops and gardens. These green spaces provide a habitat for wildlife, reduce energy consumption, and enhance the aesthetic appeal of the city. Some of these rooftops even produce organic vegetables, contributing to local urban farming projects.

Fact 73: The Paris Agreement on Climate Change

The Paris Agreement, signed in 2015, is a landmark global effort to combat climate change. As the host city, Paris plays a significant symbolic role in this international commitment to reducing greenhouse gas emissions and limiting global temperature rise. The agreement has inspired many of the city's own environmental policies, making Paris a leader in sustainability.

Fact 74: The Seine River Clean-Up Projects

Paris has launched several clean-up projects to restore the health of the Seine River. These efforts aim to reduce pollution and improve water quality, with a goal of making the river safe for swimming by the 2024 Olympics. The projects also include creating riverbanks for pedestrians and cyclists, promoting recreation alongside ecological efforts.

Fact 75: Paris's Electric Car-Sharing Program

Paris has implemented an electric car-sharing program to promote sustainable transportation. This initiative allows residents and visitors to rent electric vehicles on a short-term basis, helping reduce the city's carbon footprint and traffic congestion. The program is part of Paris's broader plan to decrease the number of private vehicles and promote greener alternatives for getting around the city.

Chapter 17: Paris and Technology

- Fact 76: Paris's Growing Tech Scene

- Fact 77: Paris as a Smart City

- Fact 78: Electric Vehicles in Paris

- Fact 79: Paris and 5G Technology

- Fact 80: Tech Conferences and Events in Paris

Fact 76: Paris's Growing Tech Scene

Paris has become a hub for technology and innovation, with a booming start-up culture and several tech incubators. The city hosts Station F, one of the largest start-up campuses in the world, attracting entrepreneurs and investors from across the globe. Paris is steadily gaining recognition as a key player in the global tech industry, thanks to its dynamic ecosystem and supportive infrastructure. The city's vibrant tech scene is fostering new ideas and driving forward technological advancements.

Fact 77: Paris as a Smart City

Paris is embracing the concept of a "smart city," integrating digital technologies to improve urban life. From intelligent traffic management systems to smart street lighting and data-driven urban planning, the city is using technology to enhance sustainability and efficiency. This approach helps improve public services and reduce the city's environmental impact.

Fact 78: Electric Vehicles in Paris

Paris is at the forefront of electric vehicle adoption, with initiatives to reduce emissions and improve air quality. The city has introduced electric car-sharing programs and is expanding charging infrastructure to encourage the use of electric vehicles. This shift is part of a larger effort to make Paris a more sustainable and eco-friendly city.

Fact 79: Paris and 5G Technology

Paris is among the cities leading the way in the rollout of 5G technology, offering faster mobile internet and enhancing connectivity. This next-generation network will support innovation in sectors like healthcare, transportation, and urban planning. The implementation of 5G is expected to revolutionize how people interact with technology in their daily lives.

Fact 80: Tech Conferences and Events in Paris

Paris hosts several major tech conferences and events, attracting professionals and innovators from around the world. These gatherings showcase the latest advancements in tech and innovation, helping Paris remain at the forefront of global technological developments and fostering collaboration across industries.

Chapter 18: Paris by Night

- Fact 81: The Illumination of the Eiffel Tower

- Fact 82: Night Cruises on the Seine

- Fact 83: Parisian Night Markets

- Fact 84: Parisian Jazz Clubs

- Fact 85: The "City of Lights" Name Origin

Fact 81: The Illumination of the Eiffel Tower

At night, the Eiffel Tower is illuminated with thousands of sparkling lights, creating a dazzling display that lasts for five minutes every hour after sunset. This light show has become one of Paris's most iconic nighttime attractions, drawing visitors from around the world to witness the tower's breathtaking glow.

Fact 82: Night Cruises on the Seine

Night cruises along the Seine River offer a unique way to experience Paris's illuminated landmarks. These boat tours provide stunning views of famous sites like the Eiffel Tower, Notre-Dame Cathedral, and the Louvre, all beautifully lit against the night sky. The cruises often include commentary and sometimes dinner, enhancing the sightseeing experience.

Fact 83: Parisian Night Markets

Parisian night markets, or "marchés nocturnes," provide a vibrant shopping experience after dark. These markets often feature local produce, artisan goods, and street food, creating a lively atmosphere where visitors can enjoy Paris's culinary delights and unique finds while strolling through bustling stalls. They are also a great place to experience local culture and interact with Parisian vendors.

Fact 84: Parisian Jazz Clubs

Paris has a rich history of jazz music, with many iconic clubs that come alive after dark. Venues like Le Duc des Lombards and Caveau de la Huchette offer intimate settings where visitors can enjoy live jazz performances. These clubs showcase both local talent and international artists, reflecting Paris's longstanding appreciation for jazz and its vibrant music scene.

Fact 85: The "City of Lights" Name Origin

Paris is often called the "City of Lights" due to its early adoption of street lighting in the 17th century, which made it one of the first cities to be illuminated at night. The name also reflects the city's historical role as a center of intellectual and cultural enlightenment, symbolizing the spread of ideas and knowledge. Today, the glowing skyline continues to enchant visitors, maintaining Paris's reputation as a beacon of culture and innovation.

Chapter 19: IShopping in Paris

- Fact 86: The Famous Champs-Élysées Shopping Street

- Fact 87: Parisian Flea Markets

- Fact 88: Les Galeries Lafayette Department Store

- Fact 89: Paris's Perfume Industry

- Fact 90: Designer Fashion Houses in Paris

Fact 86: The Famous Champs-Élysées Shopping Street

The Champs-Élysées is one of Paris's most iconic shopping streets, renowned for its luxury boutiques, flagship stores, and vibrant atmosphere. Stretching from the Arc de Triomphe to Place de la Concorde, it offers a mix of high-end fashion, popular brands, and cafes, making it a must-visit for shoppers and tourists alike. The avenue also hosts annual events and parades, adding to its allure and cultural significance.

Fact 87: Parisian Flea Markets

Paris is home to several renowned flea markets, such as the Marché aux Puces de Saint-Ouen, which is one of the largest antique markets in the world. These markets offer a treasure trove of vintage clothing, antiques, and unique collectibles, providing an eclectic shopping experience and a glimpse into Paris's history and culture. Strolling through these markets is not only about shopping but also about discovering hidden gems and engaging with local vendors.

Fact 88: Les Galeries Lafayette Department Store

Les Galeries Lafayette is a historic department store located on Boulevard Haussmann, famous for its stunning glass dome and extensive selection of fashion, beauty products, and gourmet foods. The store's architectural beauty and wide range of high-end and designer brands make it a shopping destination and a cultural landmark in Paris. Visitors can also enjoy panoramic views of the city from the store's rooftop terrace, offering a unique perspective of Paris.

Fact 89: Paris's Perfume Industry

Paris has a long-standing reputation as a global center for perfume production and innovation. The city is home to some of the world's most prestigious perfume houses, offering exclusive fragrances and bespoke creations. Parisian perfume shops and boutiques provide a unique shopping experience, showcasing a wide variety of scents and luxurious blends.

Fact 90: Designer Fashion Houses in Paris

Paris is synonymous with high fashion and is the headquarters of many of the world's leading designer fashion houses. The city hosts numerous fashion boutiques and ateliers where visitors can explore the latest collections and experience the cutting edge of global fashion trends. Paris Fashion Week, held twice a year, further solidifies the city's status as the global capital of haute couture.

Chapter 20: Paris Fun Facts

- Fact 91: Paris Once Had a "Mountain" of Wine
- Fact 92: Paris's Oldest Bridge is Called "New Bridge"
- Fact 93: There's a Hidden Vineyard in Montmartre

- Fact 94: Parisian Street Signs Were Once Made of Marble

- Fact 95: Paris Has an Official "Smell" Designer

Fact 91: Paris Once Had a "Mountain" of Wine

In the 17th century, Paris had what was known as the "Montagne de la Faveur," or the "Mountain of Wine." This wasn't an actual mountain but rather a massive pile of barrels filled with wine stored in the city. Wine merchants brought their goods from surrounding regions to Paris, where the wine was stored in large quantities, creating what looked like a mountain of barrels. Wine has always been a vital part of Parisian culture, and many homes had their own small wine cellars!

Fact 92: Paris's Oldest Bridge is Called "New Bridge"

The oldest standing bridge in Paris is ironically called Pont Neuf, which means "New Bridge" in French. Built in 1607, Pont Neuf crosses the Seine River and is known for its unique design, which included sidewalks, a novel concept at the time. Despite its name, it's actually the oldest bridge still in use in Paris today. Visitors can stroll across this historic bridge to enjoy some of the best views of the river and the Île de la Cité.

Fact 93: There's a Hidden Vineyard in Montmartre

Tucked away in the famous Montmartre neighborhood is a hidden vineyard called Clos Montmartre. This small vineyard, located near the Sacré-Cœur Basilica, has been producing wine since the 1930s. Despite Paris being a bustling city, this vineyard continues to produce a limited amount of wine each year. While the wine itself may not be world-famous, the vineyard is a charming reminder of Montmartre's agricultural past and the importance of wine in French culture.

Fact 94:Parisian Street Signs Were Once Made of Marble

In the 18th and 19th centuries, Parisian street signs were made from marble. These luxurious street signs were hand-carved with the names of streets and placed on buildings. While most have been replaced by modern metal signs, a few of these beautiful old marble signs can still be found in the city, especially in historic districts like Le Marais. They are a fascinating reminder of the attention to detail that Paris has always given to its public spaces.

Fact 95: Paris Has an Official "Smell" Designer

Did you know that Paris has an official "smell designer"? The city takes the aroma of its public spaces so seriously that it hired a perfumer to help manage its olfactory environment. The designer works to ensure that certain areas of the city have pleasant smells, from the scent of flowers in parks to the fragrances in public transport stations. This is part of Paris's unique charm, ensuring that every sense, including smell, contributes to the overall experience of the city.

Chapter 21 : Future Prospects

- Fact 96: Technological Advancements - Paris's Tech Scene and Startups
- Fact 97: Sustainable Development - Eco-Friendly Projects and Urban Planning
- Fact 98: Educational Reforms - Innovations in Education and Learning Centers
- Fact 99: Economic Growth - Paris as a Global Financial Hub
- Fact 100: Taiwan's Role in the Global Community

Fact 96: Technological Advancements - Paris's Tech Scene and Startups

Paris is rapidly becoming a hub for technology and innovation, with its thriving tech scene and startup ecosystem. The city is home to Station F, the world's largest startup campus, which hosts hundreds of innovative companies and entrepreneurs. Paris also excels in fields like artificial intelligence, biotechnology, and fintech. The French government has invested heavily in fostering innovation, leading to Paris's emergence as a key player in the global tech industry.

Fact 97: Sustainable Development - Eco-Friendly Projects and Urban Planning

Paris is leading the way in sustainable development, with a focus on creating greener, more eco-friendly spaces. The city has implemented numerous urban planning projects to reduce carbon emissions, including expanding its bicycle lanes and developing green rooftops. Initiatives like the transformation of the Seine River banks into pedestrian-friendly areas showcase the city's commitment to sustainability and environmental protection.

Fact 98: Educational Reforms - Innovations in Education and Learning Centers

Paris is pushing the boundaries of education with innovative reforms and the development of cutting-edge learning centers. Schools and universities in Paris are embracing technology to enhance the learning experience. Programs that encourage creativity and entrepreneurship are shaping the future generation of leaders.

Fact 99: Economic Growth - Paris as a Global Financial Hub

Paris is not just a cultural capital but also a major player in the world economy. The city is a global financial hub, with many of the world's leading banks, insurance companies, and multinational corporations headquartered here. Paris's stock exchange, Euronext Paris, is one of the largest in Europe. The city's strong infrastructure, along with its strategic position in the European Union, continues to attract significant foreign investment, boosting its economic growth and influence.

Fact 100: Taiwan's Role in the Global Community

While Paris continues to grow as an international hub, Taiwan plays a unique role in the global community. Taiwan has become a key partner in areas like technology, trade, and education. Collaborations between Paris and Taiwan, particularly in tech industries like semiconductors and AI, have strengthened over the years. Taiwan's presence in global markets and its contributions to sustainable development and innovation position it as an important player on the world stage.

Conclusion

Well done, young explorers! You've discovered 100 amazing facts about the magical city of Paris. From famous landmarks to hidden treasures, you've learned what makes Paris truly special.

But the adventure isn't over! Whether you dream of visiting the Eiffel Tower or strolling by the Seine, Paris is always waiting for you. Keep exploring, and one day, you might create your own stories in the City of Light!

Merci, and see you next time!